Montessori Autumn Workbook

A Montessori Book For Pre-K & K. Worksheets + Activities + Paper Materials. Maths, Alphabet, Numbers, Objects, Animals. Full Colour

Table of Contents

ACTIVITY 1

Autumn Scene Photograph Matching

1. Cut out the images.

2. Present your child with two sets of 12 cards. One of the sets contains square photographs. The second set of cards contains circles with a small section of these photographs.

3. Your child can match the square photographs with the circles.

PECKSNIFFS

ACTIVITY 2

Ranking Fall Colors

1. On the next page you'll find three color palettes. Cut out each of the rectangles.
2. Present your child with the five colors that belong to one color palette.
3. Ask your child to grade the colors from darkest to lightest shade.

ACTIVITY 3

Autumn Go-Togethers

1. Cut out the images.

2. Present your child with two sets of 8 cards. One set contains photographs. The other set contains isolated objects that match the scenes on the photographs.

3. Your child can match one card in the set to a card from the other set.

Royal
0.99

ACTIVITY 4

Beginning Sounds

Draw a line to match the beginning sound of the image on the left to a letter on the right.

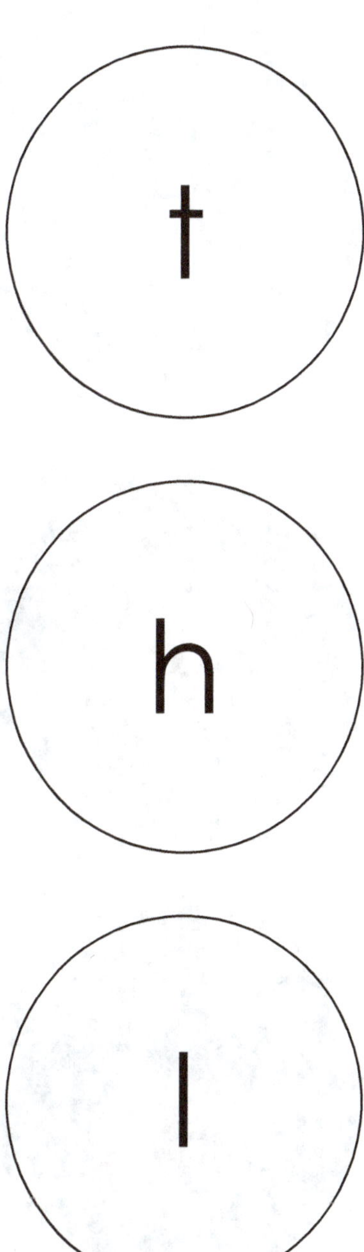

t

h

l

ACTIVITY 4

Beginning Sounds

Draw a line to match the beginning sound of the image on the left to a letter on the right.

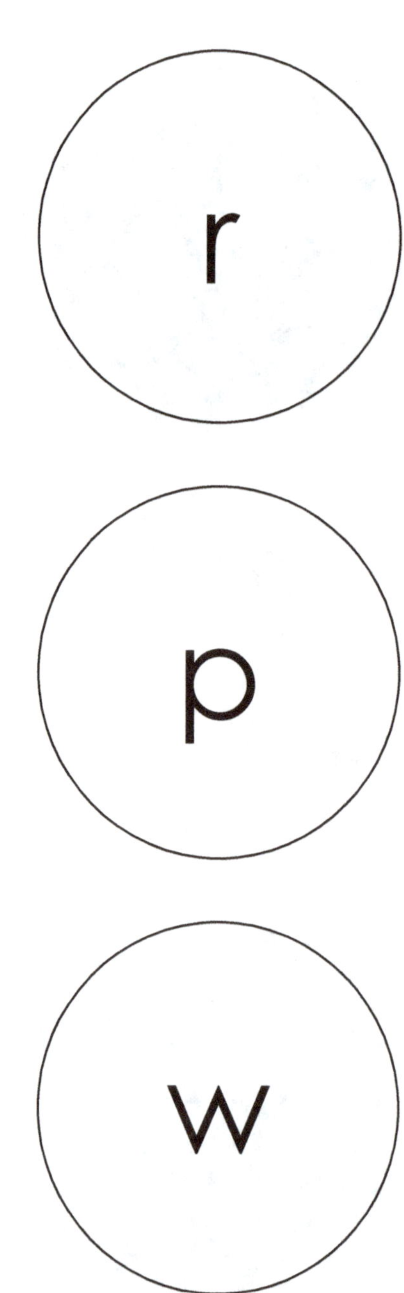

r

p

w

ACTIVITY 4

Beginning Sounds

Draw a line to match the beginning sound of the image on the left to a letter on the right.

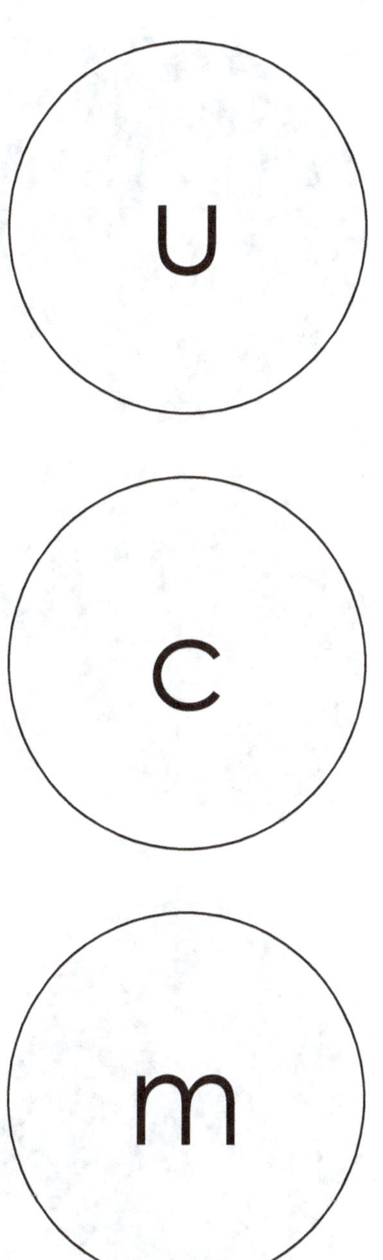

u

c

m

ACTIVITY 4

Beginning Sounds

Draw a line to match the beginning sound of the image on the left to a letter on the right.

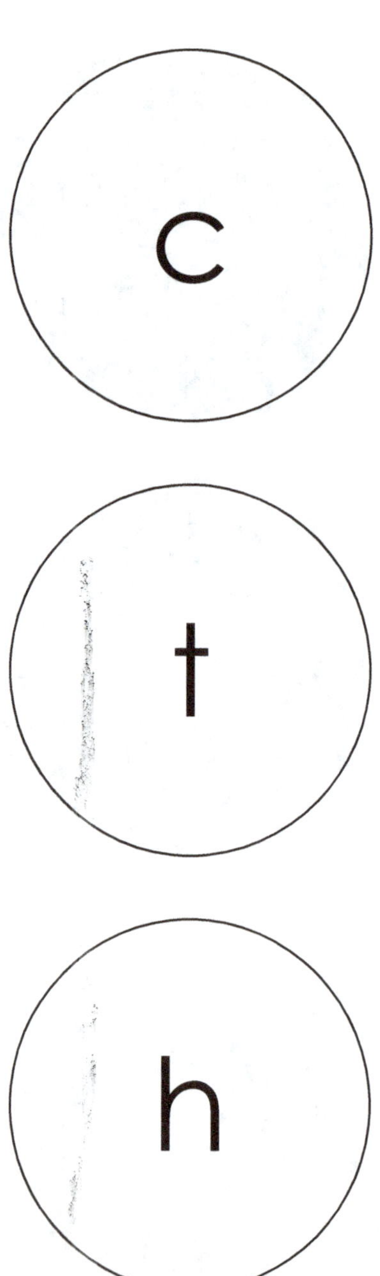

c

t

h

ACTIVITY 4

Beginning Sounds

Draw a line to match the beginning sound of the image on the left to a letter on the right.

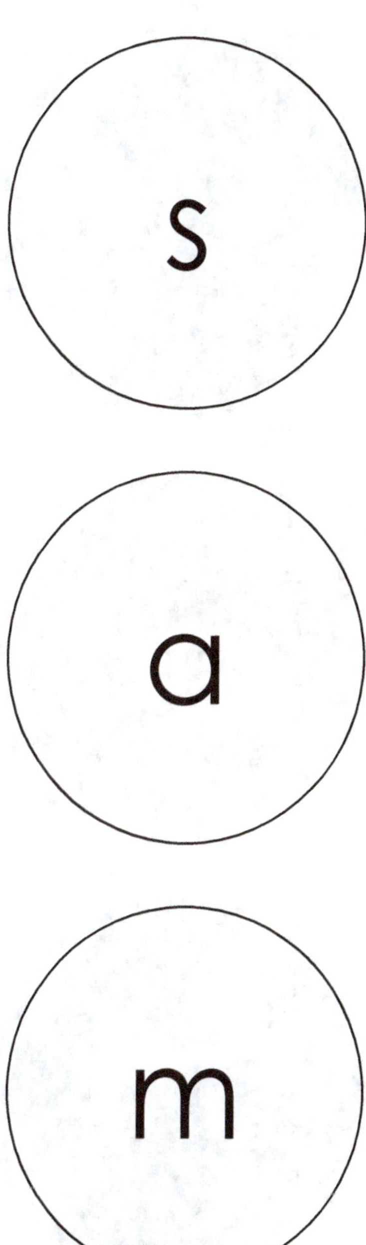

s

a

m

ACTIVITY 4

Beginning Sounds

Draw a line to match the beginning sound of the image on the left to a letter on the right.

h

d

c

ACTIVITY 4

Beginning Sounds

Draw a line to match the beginning sound of the image on the left to a letter on the right.

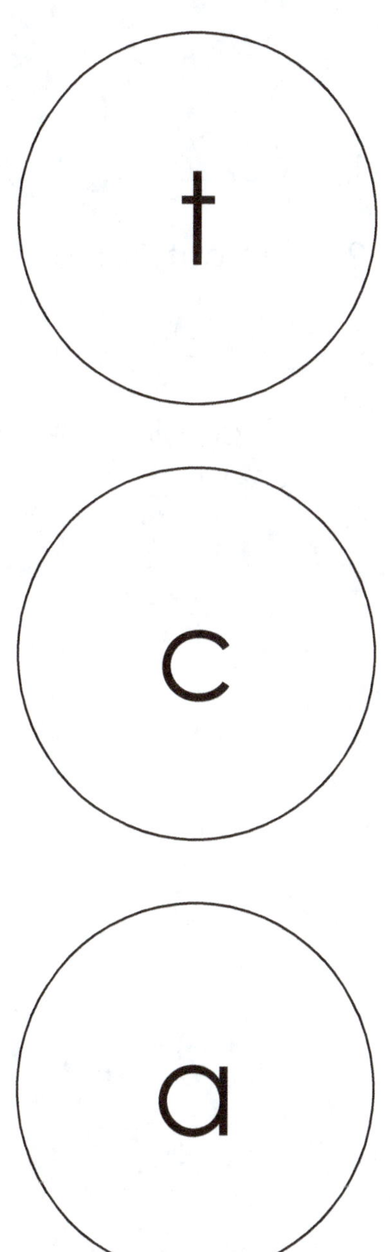

t

c

a

ACTIVITY 5

Missing Leaf Numbers

1. Cut out the images.
2. Put out five rows of numbers and five separate leafs that match.
3. Your child can match the leafs to the missing numbers in the row.
4. Since all of the numbers will be used up, there is a built-in control of error.

4
2
1

5
4
3

7
6
4

7
6
5

10
8
7

3

6

5

8

9

13
12
10

15
14
13

15
14
13

18
16
15

20
19
17

11

12

16

17

18

ACTIVITY 6

Pumpkin Pinprick

Use a large pushpin to punch holes in the dots around the shape. The goal is to cut the shape out of the paper without scissors. It's helpful to put the paper on some cork and pin it down at the corners to keep it in place.

ACTIVITY 7

Life Cycle of a Turkey

1. Cut out the cards.
2. Your child can line up the cards in the correct order of the life cycle.
3. Optional: if you have a miniature version of a turkey, place this with the cards as well to bring the activity to life.

egg

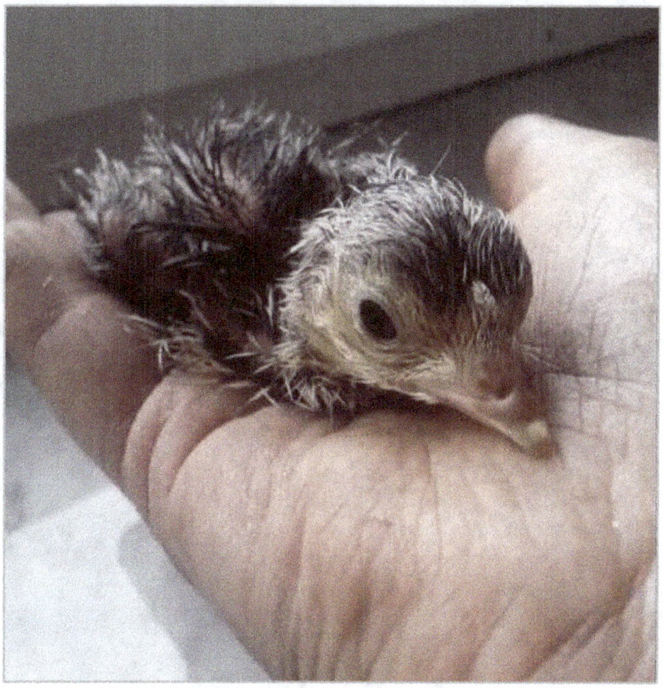

hatchling

poult

adult turkey

ACTIVITY 8

Fall Leaf Cutting Strips

1. Cut out the three strips.
2. Your child can practice cutting along the dotted line to the illustration.

CUT OUT

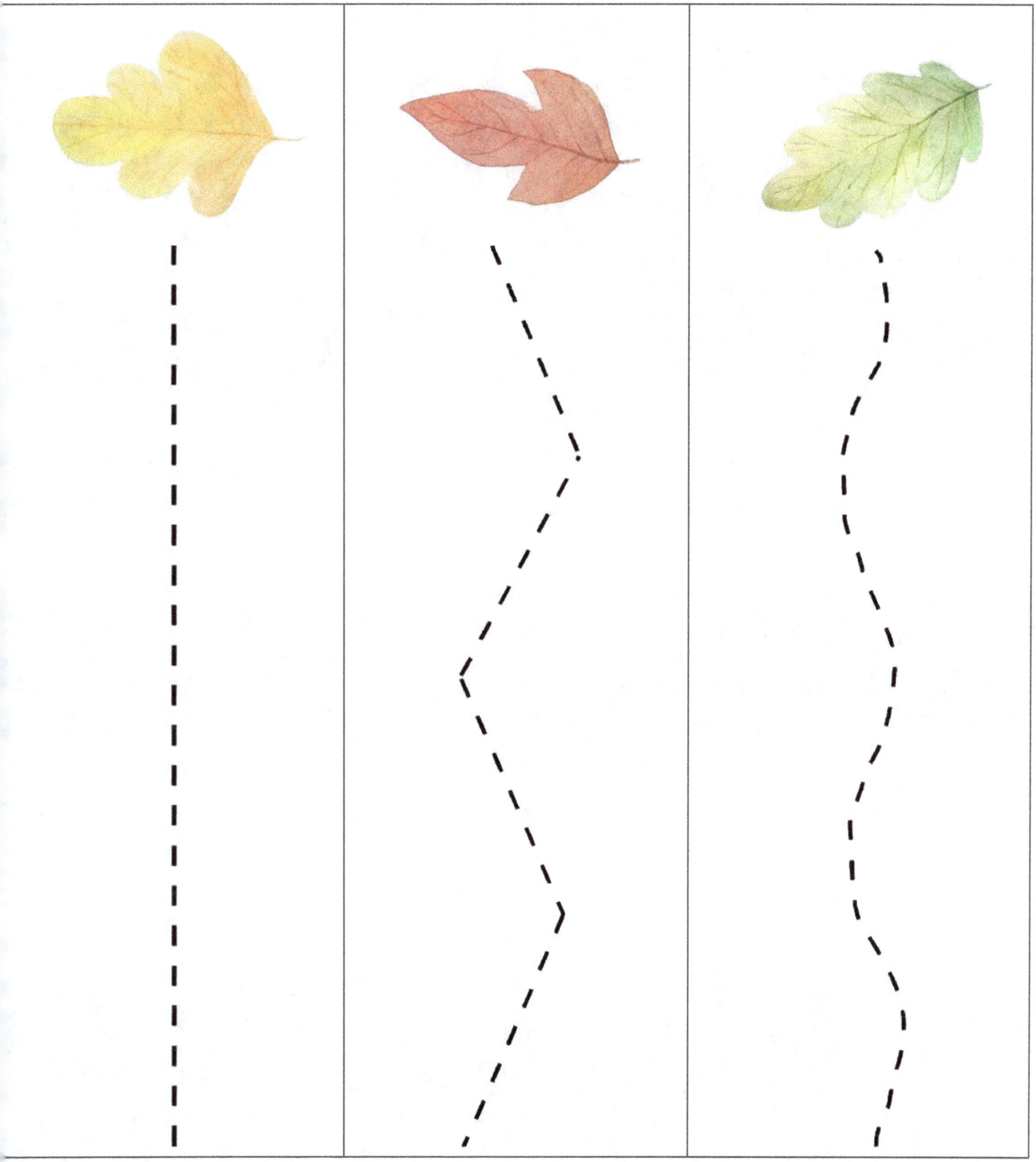

ACTIVITY 9

Rhyming Riddles

1. Cut out the picture and riddle cards.
2. Present the picture cards to your child. Make sure it's clear to him or her what is displayed.
3. Read the riddle aloud to your child. Ask him or her to match it to a picture card.

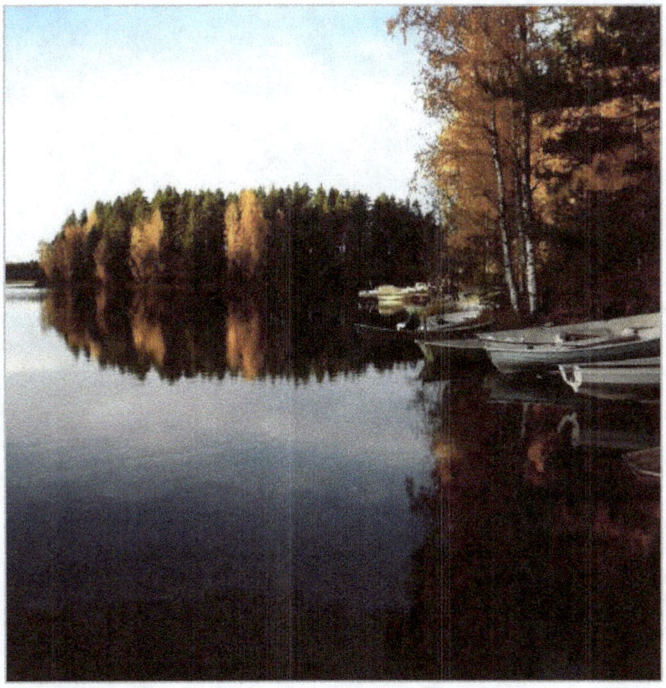

I rhyme with “cake”.

I am a ______ (lake).

I rhyme with “brain”.

I am a ______ (train).

I rhyme with "root".

I am a ______ (boot).

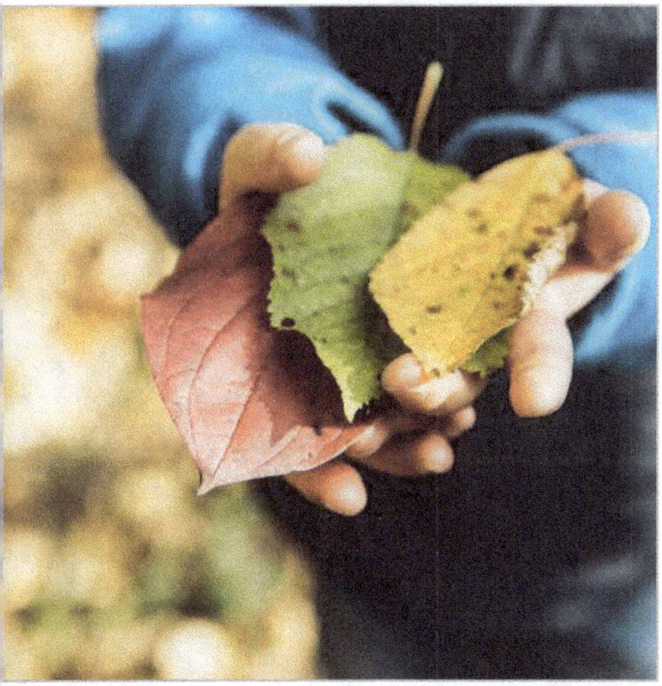

I rhyme with "chief".

I am a ______ (leaf).

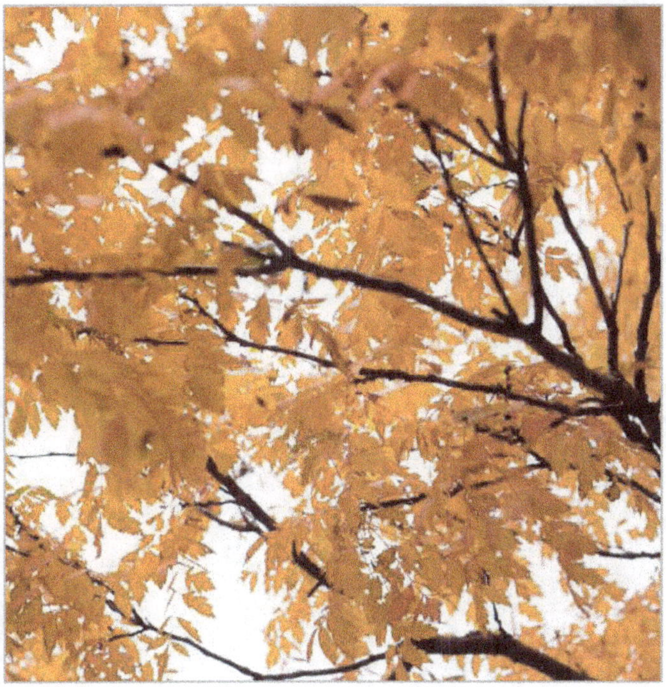

I rhyme with "free".

I am a ______ (tree).

I rhyme with "fridge".

I am a ______ (bridge).

I rhyme with "quirky".

I am a ______ (turkey).

I rhyme with "rock".

I am a ______ (sock).

ACTIVITY 10

Leaf Lacing Card

1. Cut out the leaf.
2. Use a hole punch to create holes along the outline of the shape, about an inch apart.
3. Your child can lace the shape using a shoelace or a blunt needle with some yarn.

ACTIVITY 11

Acorn Counting

1. Cut out the number cards. No need to cut out the tree from the page.
2. You can use the paper acorns, but it's even more fun to use a basket of 10 actual acorns instead.
3. Place the number cards in random order face down in a pile. Gather your basket of acorns. Place the page with the tree next to it.
4. Your child can draw a number card, count out the correct number of acorns and place them on the tree.

1	2	3
4	5	6
7	8	9
10		

CUT OUT

ACTIVITY 12

Fall Pattern Strips

1. Cut out the eight strips and the eight separate cards.
2. Present all of the material to your child. Or, to make it easier at first, just take four strips and four (matching) separate cards.
3. Your child can find the image that's supposed to come next on a strip based on the sequencing of the images.
4. Once the work is complete, all of the separate cards should have been matched, creating a built-in control of error.

CUT OUT

ACTIVITY 13

Autumn Plant or Animal?

1. Cut out the cards.

2. Lay out the cover cards with the text "plant" and "animal". Put the picture cards in a little basket next to it.

3. Your child can determine for each card whether a plant or an animal is pictured and put it next to the cover card.

plant

animal

plant or animal?

plant or animal?

plant or animal?

plant or animal?

plant or animal?

plant or animal?

plant or animal?

plant or animal?

plant or animal?

plant or animal?

plant or animal?

plant or animal?

plant or animal?

plant or animal?

plant or animal?

plant or animal?

plant or animal?

plant or animal?

plant or animal?

plant or animal?

ACTIVITY 14

Autumn Living or Non-living?

1. Cut out the cards.

2. Lay out the cover cards with the text "living" and "non-living". Put the picture cards in a little basket next to it.

3. Your child can determine for each card whether a living or a non-living thing is pictured and put it next to the cover card.

living	non-living

living or non-living?

living or non-living?

living or non-living?

living or non-living?

living or non-living?

living or non-living?

living or non-living?

living or non-living?

living or non-living?

living or non-living?

living or non-living?

living or non-living?

living or non-living?

living or non-living?

living or non-living?

living or non-living?

living or non-living?

living or non-living?

living or non-living?

living or non-living?

ACTIVITY 15

Fall Size Sorting Jars

1. Cut out the circles with the images. No need to cut out the jars.

2. Your child can sort the images: the big ones go into the big jar and the small ones go into the small jar.

3. You could present all of the images at once, or you could only lay out only one of the shapes first, depending on what challenge suits your child's age.

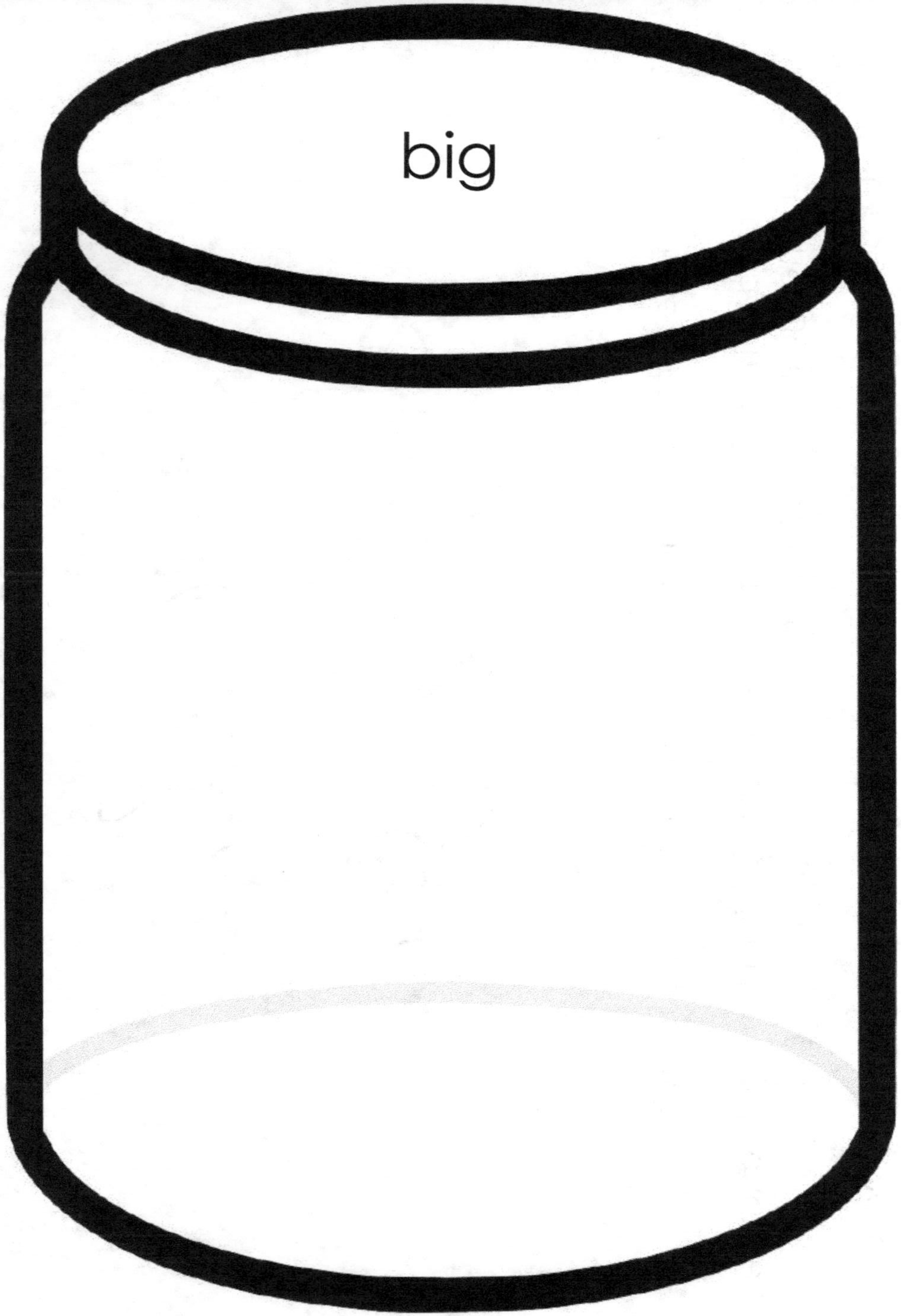
big

small

ACTIVITY 16

Autumn or Spring?

Draw a line to match each picture to the season it belongs to: autumn or spring?

autumn

spring

ACTIVITY 16

Autumn or Spring?

Draw a line to match each picture to the season it belongs to: autumn or spring?

autumn

spring

ACTIVITY 17

Autumn Counting

How many can you count?

ACTIVITY 17

Autumn Counting

How many can you count?

 ________  ________  ________

ACTIVITY 17

Autumn Counting

How many can you count?

 ____________  ____________  ____________

ACTIVITY 18

Fall Silhouettes

Draw a line to match the animal on the left to its silhouette on the right.

ACTIVITY 19

Squirrel Labyrinth

Draw a line to let the squirrel run to the nut. Try not to bump into the edges!

ACTIVITY 20

Autumn 3 Part Cards

Cut out the cards so that you have 1) pictures with labels, 2) pictures without labels and 3) labels.

There are many ways to use these cards. Some examples:

- Use the picture cards as flashcards.
- Use the picture cards with labels to play a game like I spy. E.g. "I spy with my little eye a fall item that starts with the sound "ssss".
- Let kids match the picture cards with the labels, using the pictures with labels as control cards to check their own work.

leaf

leaf

corn

corn

squirrel

squirrel

acorn

acorn

pumpkin

pumpkin

tractor

tractor

umbrella

umbrella

yarn

yarn

ACTIVITY 21

Fall Subtraction

How many pictures remain?

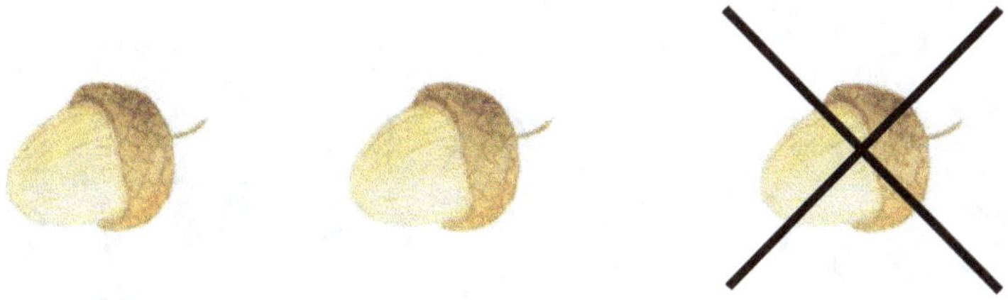

3 - 1 = ______

4 - 2 = ______

3 - 2 = ______

5 - 3 = ______

ACTIVITY 21

Fall Subtraction

How many pictures remain?

2 - 1 = ______

4 - 2 = ______

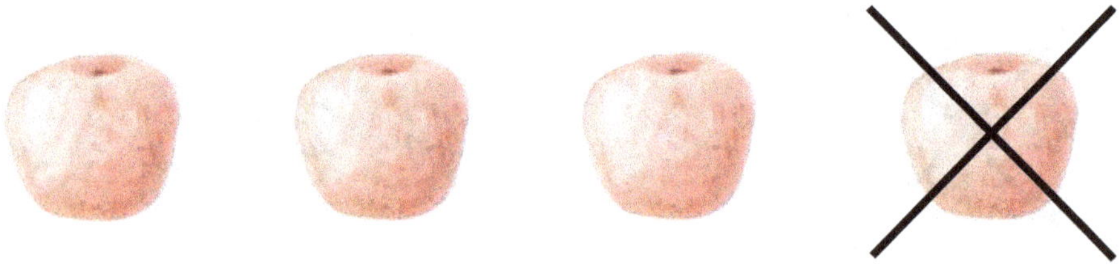

4 - 1 = ______

5 - 2 = ______

ACTIVITY 22

Autumn Item Color Matching

1. Cut out the color cards and the picture circles.

2. Your child can sort the pictures by color and put them next to the color cards. You can present your child with as many pictures as you feel are the right challenge.

red

green

yellow

blue

ACTIVITY 23

Fall Halves

Draw a line to match the half animal on the left to its match on the right.

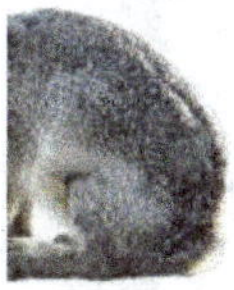

ACTIVITY 24

Let's Make 10

Draw more to make 10. Finish the addition equation.

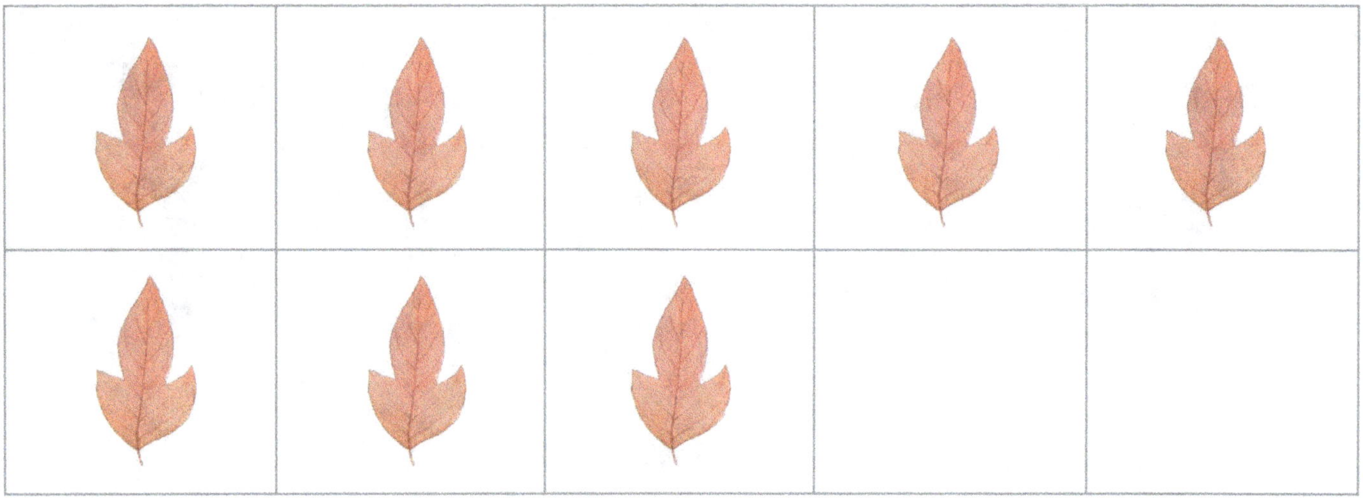

8 + _____ = 10

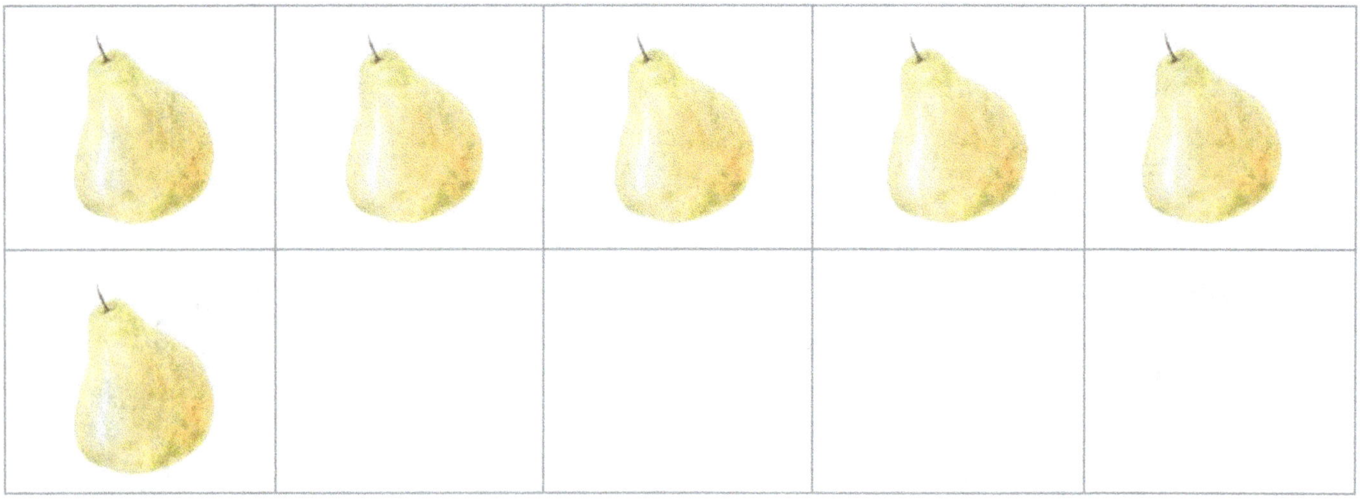

6 + _____ = 10

ACTIVITY 24

Let's Make 10

Draw more to make 10. Finish the addition equation.

7 + _____ = 10

4 + _____ = 10

ACTIVITY 24

Let's Make 10

Draw more to make 10. Finish the addition equation.

3 + _____ = 10

9 + _____ = 10

ACTIVITY 25

Autumn Pattern Matching

1. Cut out the images.
2. For each of the illustrations there are nine cards with three different patterns.
3. Present your child with the nine cards of one illustration.
4. Ask your child to find the matching patterns (instead of the matching colors).

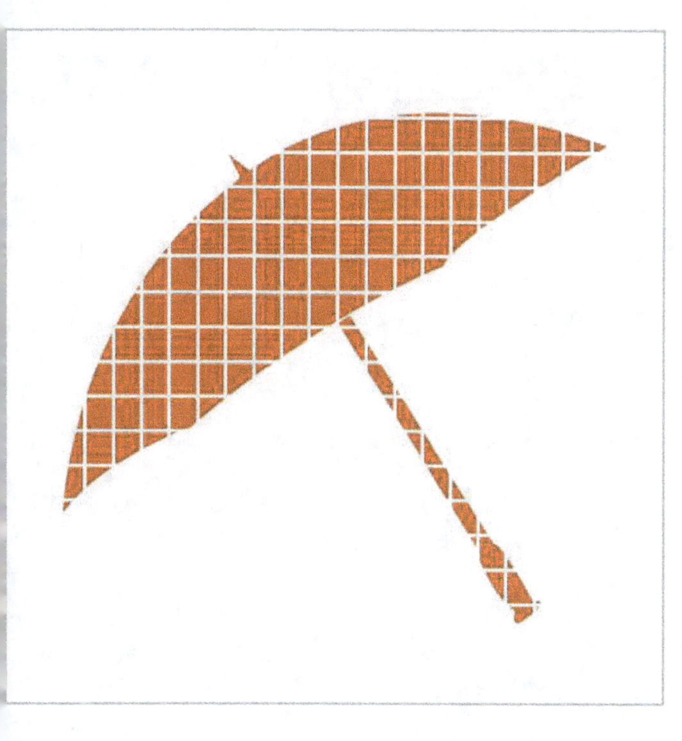

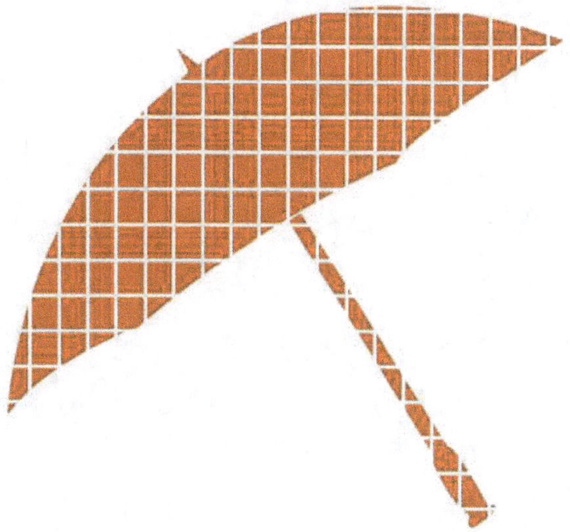

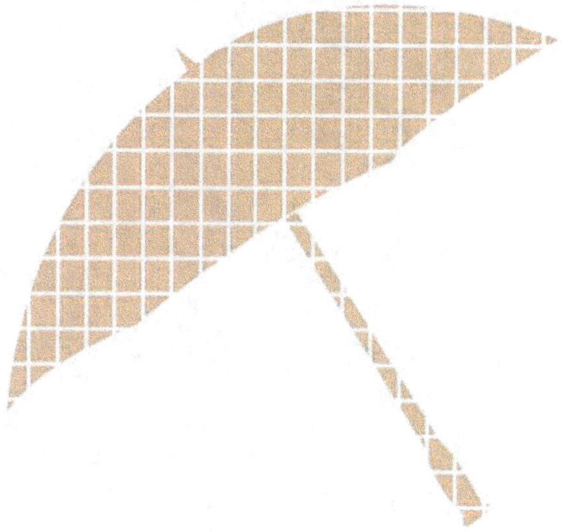

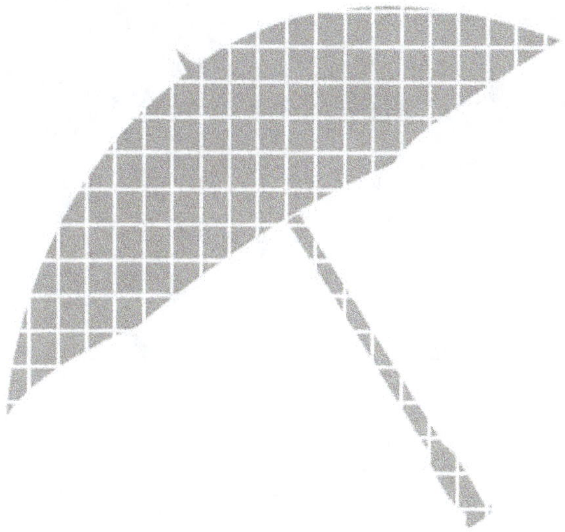

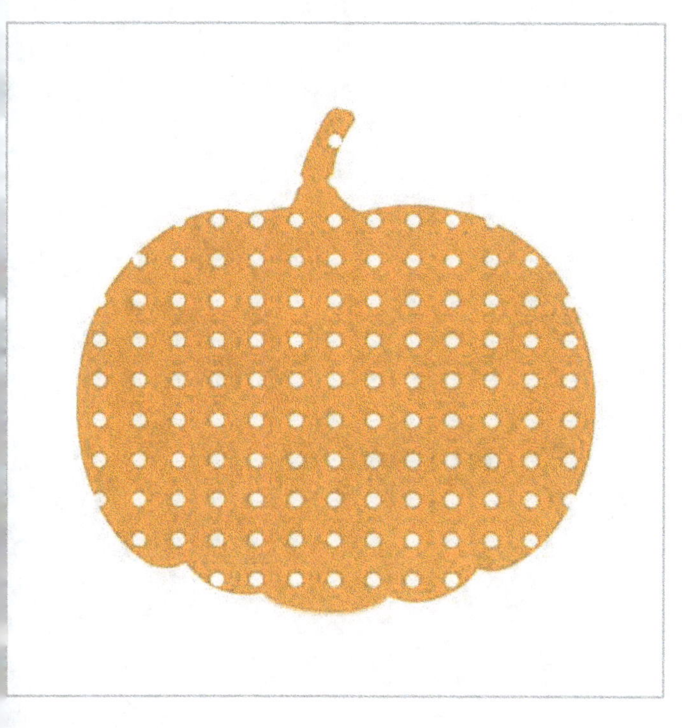

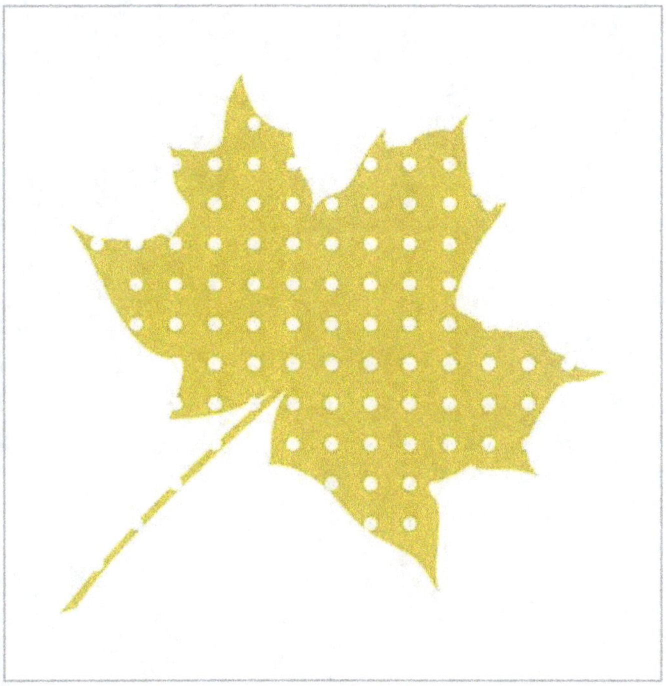

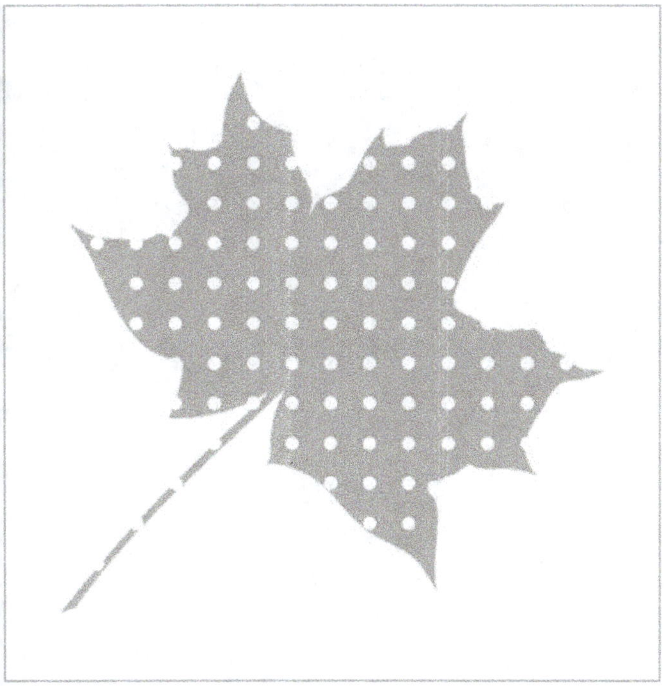

www.ingramcontent.com/pod-product-compliance
Lightning Source LLC
Chambersburg PA
CBHW080447030726
47592CB00011B/3005
9781803611488